Marc Adams

Marc Adams (lost)Found

Marc Adams (2005)

Date   Name & email or phone

Published by Window Books

Marc Adams
PO Box 495
Seattle WA 98111

www.meetmarcadams.com
marc@meetmarcadams.com

www.heartstrong.org
heartstrong@heartstrong.org

ISBN 1-889829-10-2

This is a nonfiction book.
To protect anonymity, some names have been changed and some
situations differ slightly from original occurrence.

Lyrics to *Long After Tomorrow (pages 123, 124)* reprinted with
permission. Written by Julie Flanders and Emil Adler. Copyright
1992. www.octoberproject.net

Published in the United States of America.

for the one who proved to me
that everything I believed
about love was true

I believe love can only grow if it changes.
I wish childhood came after adulthood.
I think about love almost all the time.
I'm afraid to give up.
I know I am hopelessly in love with him.

I believe it is too late for complacency.
I wish we had the promise of tomorrow.
I think he knew it the first time he saw me.
I'm afraid I might have to fight back.
I know I can save someone today.

"Love is never wrong."

I cringed the first time I heard that sentence. It was a difficult concept for me. Even after over a decade of recuperating from my vicious upbringing as a fundamentalist Baptist Christian, occasionally, I found myself recoiling from new concepts.

I always assumed that if I felt love for someone that it was respectable. As long as it fit within the reflections from the heterosexual mirror before which I continuously positioned my very homosexual life.

Yet, suddenly, there was this statement in this poem being read by a teenage boy who shared my history.

As I began to examine the ramifications of respecting that statement, I began an inward journey. A journey that allowed me to once again to pick up my pen, (okay, sit down at my computer) and open my kimono to the world.

When I sat down to begin sharing about the love in my life it was difficult to know where to start. After getting a poem from a boyfriend thousands of miles from me, I realized exactly what it was that I would write about and how I would do it. This book is the result of that poem and a result of a few other significant persons in my life that I have loved and who have loved me.

Many people think that they know everything about my life because they have heard me speak or read *The Preacher's Son* or my poetry books. While I spent hours agonizing over the parts of my life that I wished to reveal to the world in the past, I am still (sometimes painfully) aware that I have not shared enough.

Over the course of the past eight years I have met countless men and women who have asked for more. I searched through the 250 pages I edited out of *The Preacher's Son* and my poetry books looking for what else I could share and I tried to recall what new parts of my life I could bare to the world.

In my searching, I realized that there was much to share. There were pieces of my life that were so precious to me that I had feared sharing them with strangers. (I know, it might be hard to believe that if you have read *The Preacher's Son*.) There was love in my life that I was finally ready to share with those who cared to understand it.

That is what this book is really all about. And, as I once again, open my kimono to the world, I am still not perfect in my process. Often, I am still the teenage boy wandering through his life searching. Every day I remind myself that I am still that boy and that, gladly, this searching will not end.

For some, this book will provide fodder for criticism and judgment as I discovered with each of my previous books. I am so beyond doing things to please other people at this point in my life that I decided that I didn't even need to try with these pages. I chose to make everything about this book unconventional. Perhaps that makes this book less commercial than *The Preacher's Son*, but it is the best way for me to convey my thoughts.

I have found in my journey that what a few people criticize me for most is what most people find so inviting.

For me, the process of living is not an existence in a stagnant pool but an evolving progression of discovery and inclusion. It is out of that discovery and inclusion that I found the courage to write on these blank pages. For me, this is not just writing but responsibility. For love is not just given but also taken.

If you take anything from the words on these pages I hope it is insight to find the greatest gift that was given to you. The gift of living and loving. Loving ourselves first and then loving others. No one should live a life alone. We have love in our hearts so that we can give it away. I started with myself and then began with others. That's why love is never wrong.

I believe God would not use pain to teach us
about love.
I wish I had more time.
I think about sex a lot.
I'm afraid I'm a bad kisser.
I know tomorrow I will love him even more.

I believe it takes only one person to make a family.
I wish I'd never lied.
I think every heart needs a second chance.
I'm afraid no one will take up my work
when I am done.
I know God would be much bigger than
Jerry Falwell taught me.

Part One

She used to sleep with me every night. Her body next to mine was wonderful and calming.

Every night, before I would go to sleep, I would call her name. Within moments, she would come into my room and look up at me with the sweetest eyes. I would caress the beautiful, silky black hair on her head. When I would lie down on my bed she would lie down next to me. I always slept on my back and she would move over to me and rest her head on my shoulder.

I would always kiss her head and she would rest her body weight against me. She would breathe deeply and within seconds, would be fast asleep. If she didn't snore so loudly, I could have slept the entire night just being close to her.

I had spent most of my life wanting someone like her. Even as a boy, I dreamed of having someone like her with whom to share my life. I needed someone just like her to listen to my sadness and my happiness. I wondered what it would be like to have a constant companion full of acceptance, who would be there no matter what. It took me until I was 19, but when I saw her I knew she was the one.

Her name was Ashley. I named her that because of the splash of grayish, silverish hair on her chest which was otherwise covered with beautiful, silky, black fur. She was the perfect cocker spaniel.

After leaving college, I decided that I wanted to share my life with someone other than my family and myself. That's when I found Ashley. She helped me think about someone other than myself.

Fifteen years later, Ashley was long gone, but I found my second and third dogs. My boyfriend and I found them at an animal shelter in Seattle. After Todd's inspection and approval, we took them from their impending, unspeakable doom and added them to our growing family of choice.

They were throw away dogs who, in many ways, reminded me of the throw away young people I've dedicated my life to reaching and supporting.

After a few days of living with Rufus and Goofy, I found the same calming effect I had experienced with Ashley. They taught me more about love when I thought I already knew everything. Most of the time they love me more than I think I love myself.

I never even thought about loving myself until I was twenty-three years old. My former religion pretty much stole my self esteem and freedom to think for myself. Most of my childhood and young adulthood was scorched by the fire of my self-censuring beliefs.

The mere thought of having the freedom to love myself was demonic and unacceptable to a God whom I believed valued holiness and obedience above everything else. My teenage years were not only filled with angst and stunted personal development, but were also a time when I learned to *un*love myself.

The process was simple. All I had to do was believe the church hymns I sang almost every day of my life. Reading, singing and believing lyrics that described every human being as a wretch, a worm, and an unworthy sinner made it simple for me to believe that I was one. How could I possibly love myself if I was a completely unlovable and undeserving human being as described in *Amazing Grace*? The answer was that I couldn't love myself. I wasn't supposed to love myself. I was supposed to redefine the word love and ignore the face in the mirror. That made it easier to accept all the rest.

Somewhere inside, I have to believe that we are born with the ability to love ourselves regardless of what our parents and teachers and friends and religion and fashion magazines tell us. For most gay men I know, all those things *and* the bathroom mirror changes us. Countless hours spent analyzing ourselves and comparing our features to those deemed acceptable at that moment deprive us of seeing ourselves.

For me, I learned that at a very early age through my former religion. Fundamentalist Baptist Christianity was my birthright and for the first twenty-three years of my life, I clung to it. Everyone I spent time with, everything I saw, read, loved, or yearned for reflected what I believed was truth. My discovery of what I thought was truth was more an absorption instead of a discovery. But I believed it anyway. There isn't much patience for questions when you are young.

Being gay and knowing that I was gay from a very early age prevented me from moving ahead socially. I noticed my schoolmates and friends moving at a much different pace. I remember stifling my anger as I watched other kids on my school bus. I was angry because I was sure that none of them had the secret I had. Everyone else could see themselves reflected almost every moment of every day. I was sure that I was the only one who hated himself and his life. So, I found a way out.

I discovered that my religion was teaching me to die to myself. I read it in my Bible, I heard it spoken in church on Sunday and I saw other people claiming to have accomplished this feat.

If I lived and died only for the God I believed I loved, there was no need to love myself.

When I started my coming out process in 1987, I thought very little about learning to love myself as a result of my belief system. My first goal was to rid my head and heart of the lies I had not only told myself, but everyone with whom I had ever crossed paths. I knew it was important to come out and more important to make sure people knew that I was gay. I assumed everyone was assuming I was straight and that was not okay with me. Alright, maybe some people knew I was homosexual since I wasn't the butchest of boys when I was a boy. But the majority of people I had come to know in my life were assuming I was straight because that is what people do. And, I had spent years hiding and doing everything I could to support their fantasy.

What I really wanted to do in coming out was make myself an honest person. I thought that just telling people would help me as well. I was sure the emptiness I had felt my entire life was a result of my dishonesty with myself and others.

It wasn't.

I figured out it wasn't that about three years later after coming out to my family and most of my friends. The emptiness was still there. In fact, it seemed that I felt emptier than I had before coming out. I think in the back of my mind I knew that the emptiness had everything to do with me. As much as I had come out and learned self-respect, I still couldn't see myself when I looked into my heart.

I don't remember the moment when I realized that I needed to learn how to love myself. And maybe that's because there wasn't a definitive time when the answers came to me. I do know that I spent a month or so analyzing my life.

I would look in the mirror and not understand who it was in the reflection. The one thing that kept coming back to my mind was the deeply ingrained religious message of dying to me. I hadn't been to church in a couple years but I had memorized so much of the Bible and digested so much fundamentalist Baptist Christian doctrine that it was always quickly retrieved.

I couldn't help but wonder if the dying-

to-self doctrine was the reason for my emptiness. Had I killed myself so perfectly that I
was incapable of ever looking in the mirror and
seeing myself? The self-love with which I was
born couldn't be gone forever, could it?

The more time I spent asking myself
questions, the more I felt confused. So, I decided to stop asking the questions. The answers
suddenly didn't seem so important to me when
I wasn't thinking about the questions.

I was about 23 years old when I
stopped asking those questions. I remember
standing in my bathroom one morning staring
at my reflection in the mirror. I tried to see
something attractive, something lovable. Instead, I noticed every blemish on my skin. I
saw that I would probably lose my hair one
day and I wondered if I should save money
for a nose job. The mirror showed me that my
arms were scrawny and my ass was too flat.

Obviously, the self examination in the
mirror was not going to help me in my search

to learn how to love myself. So I stopped looking in the mirror and started looking at the part of myself that I couldn't see in a mirror.

I started looking at my heart and my mind. I realized that if I was ever going to be comfortable with the person I was, it would have to come from me. But the more that I looked at my heart and mind; I realized that the things I found were not very pleasant.

My heart was jaded from my life's experience already. Sometimes I felt nothing but coldness. I am sure those things were results of that wall I had built around me during my adolescence. It was so dense and impenetrable that sometimes I couldn't even get through it. I had done an exceptional job at protecting myself from pain.

The more I looked inward, the more I realized that the wall was not just protecting me from pain. It had become a tool for me to use to keep other people from seeing the pain that had already set up shop in my heart.

I really didn't like what I was keeping to myself. My parentally crushed dreams, my romantic hopes, and my desire to aggressively find what I needed most in my life had all become an internalized part of my life. I knew I had to break down that wall and free myself from my past.

The last thing I wanted to become was a guy who clung to his past brokenness and used it as an excuse not to go forward with his life. But who was I kidding? At that point, I was already well on my way to becoming that guy. It was a frightening admission.

I spent a few weeks trying to figure out how to change this part of my life. I looked for self-help books. Nothing useful there. Most of what I found seemed to encourage readers to stay in their pain and gather as many sympathetic friends around as possible to share in their misery. So, I gave up on the idea that I should seek advice from that source.

Then it hit me. I just needed to stop

doing it. I needed to just get rid of the wall around my heart. After all, it wasn't a real wall. It was just a wall in my mind. I was responsible for building it and maintaining it. So, I was responsible for eliminating it.

I needed to stop using my past as a reason not to go forward with my life as well as a reason not to love myself. It was so simple it scared me. I always anticipated that the process would be extremely lengthy and complicated. But as soon as I realized what it was that I needed to do, it was easy.

Well, *easy* might be too simplistic of a term. I still had to do it. But it was really a matter of me just refusing to maintain the wall. It fell away after a few weeks. They were some of the most uncomfortable weeks of my life so far. I had become very accustomed to believing that I was protected from pain, from life. To a certain extent, it was probably true.

However, instead of opening myself up to the opportunity for new pain I was just recycling my old pain over and over again. Each time I recycled, it became more and more a part of my being and most of it rested just under my skin.

As I went through the process of getting rid of it all, I noticed that I was pulling out things that I had assumed were just part of myself. They weren't that at all. They were just things I thought I needed to live my life.

The first thing to get thrown away was my fear of being hurt. I guess that was the biggest thing I needed to throw away. Maybe throw away isn't the right choice of words. I imagine that I will always have a fear of being hurt. What I was able to throw away was my inhibition to open myself up to new relationships for fear of being hurt.

As I worked on this process I immediately found myself feeling vulnerable. I was shedding something that truly had protected me. At the same time, I started feeling that my heart was not so heavy all the time. As I had proposed, in making myself vulnerable, I was also releasing the pain I had held inside.

After a while, it almost felt magical. I felt freedom I had never felt in my entire life.

I believe taking chances makes life better.
I wish I didn't have to cry.
I think those who disagree with me are right
half the time.
I'm afraid he won't always love me.
I know I am impatient.

I believe giving in to love is the most
important thing I've ever done.
I wish people didn't think they had to
speak for God.
I think many of us settle for less.
I'm afraid straight people will never ask gay people
what we need.
I know I cannot walk through the rest of my life
without him by my side.

Part Two

I looked at my grandmother sitting across from me. We were sitting in Denny's restaurant on Century Boulevard near the Los Angeles airport. It was November, 1992, and she had come to visit me in Los Angeles while she was on a trip to visit a friend in Phoenix.

The visit was about to end. It had been the most time I had ever spent alone with her in my life.

Growing up in my fundamentalist Baptist Christian home, none of us kids were allowed to spend more than ten minutes alone with her. She was my father's mother but as you know, my mother called all the shots.

My parents were pretty clear on their biblically-based beliefs about associating with people classified as non-believers.

When I was a child, every night we would get together as a "family" and read the King James Version of the Holy Bible and pray. We had certain people on our prayer lists that we prayed for continuously. My grandmother was one of those people.

I had to pray for her salvation from hell every night of my life. Because of that, I developed an intense fear that my grandmother would burn in hell forever if she wasn't the right kind of Christian.

My parents were sure of her plight due to the fact that she was divorced, wore pants, wore lipstick, had boyfriends and didn't seem to mind associating with other non-believers. As a result, I very rarely saw her and when I did it was highly supervised. So, I didn't know her very well.

Her trip to visit me in Los Angeles was unexpected. As I spent time with her that weekend, I realized that I really needed to come out to her. Months earlier, when I had come out to my family, my mother had made me promise not to ever tell my grandmother that I was gay.

My mother told me that it would kill my grandmother if she knew. Back then, I usually blindly trusted my mother and promised not to tell my grandmother. After all, my parents had always told us that there was no such thing as Santa Claus or the Easter Bunny so I never had reason to believe that my parent's would lie to me. (I ruined alot of kid's holiday's with that information.)

But there I was, starting a new relationship with my own grandmother and I was starting it with a lie.

I assumed that she, like most everyone else, assumed I was straight. If I didn't correct her assumption then I was lying. That is, after all, why we have to come out to people. But every time I thought about coming out to her, this movie would start playing in the back in of my head of Todd and I loading a casket in an airplane and sending my grandmother back to Pennsylvania. I imagined that I came out to her and, as my mother promised, she had died.

It was a horrific visual in my head and I didn't want to see it played out in front of me. So I decided not to tell my grandmother about who I really was. I rationalized that I was pro-tecting her.

So there we were in Denny's and she looked across at me and pointed to my hands which were folded on the table.

"I think it is really nice that you guys wear rings," she said.

Suddenly, I began to feel very uncom-fortable. I imagined that she was talking about the ring around my collar or the ring in the bath-tub back at the apartment. But I knew she was talking about the rings on our fingers.

That movie started playing in the back of my head again. I just smiled at her and changed the subject. There was no way that I was going to make that the moment that I came out to her. With my mother's warning echoing in my ears, I chickened out and took the easy road.

Two weeks later, I opened my mailbox to see a letter from my grandmother. She had finished her trip to Arizona and had returned home to Pennsylvania. In her letter, she thanked me for the hospitality and the fun we shared together for the first time.

Then came the part for which I was completely unprepared.

"When I brought up your rings in Denny's," she wrote, "I was trying to let you know that I have known since you were a little boy that when you grew up that you would be with men and not women. I want you to know that I love you still as my grandson and welcome anyone who is in your life as another grandson."

I was stunned. How could the only person in my family who wasn't supposed to be able to handle my homosexuality be the only person who could? She had apparently grown tired of me hiding myself and was making her love known to me.

I never felt real familial love in my life until then. It was truly one of the weirdest feelings I had experienced. Especially since I had never felt it before that moment.

All I kept thinking about was sitting in the same place a few months earlier reading that final letter from my father and how free I felt. With my grandmother's letter I suddenly felt a connection that I had never felt with a family member. I wasn't sure I liked it because it was so real and quite intense.

Then I found myself feeling unparalleled sadness and anger. The sadness was because I knew that I had considerable less time in my life to get to know my grandmother and create memories with the one family member who really loved me. I would have years but not the years that I should have had.

That led me to feel angry. My mother had lied to me about my grandmother's response. It was simple to understand that my mother was only looking out for her own best interests. She didn't want news of my homosexuality to get out to other family members. Maybe because she would feel embarrassed, maybe because she thought people would think she was to blame. More likely, it was because she didn't want me to receive any support, let alone familial support for living my life of alleged sin.

Having once been a believer in the same ideology and philosophy as my parents, it was pretty easy to figure them out.

I was also angry because I had been robbed of the opportunity to get to know my grandmother during my childhood. Along with all of the other things my parents had stolen from me during my youth, they had stolen my opportunities to receive my own grandmother's love.

Rather than let my sadness and anger eat me alive, which sometimes I felt it would, I decided to make the most out of the time I would have with my grandmother as part of my family of choice.

The first step was to do something to honor her. I had contemplated for about a year about changing my name. My birth name, which was not Marc Adams, was always so plain to me. So I decided to drop my first name, take my middle name, Mark, as my first name. I changed the "k" to a "c" and took my grandmother's maiden name of Adams as my new last name.

Something which I was going to do for vanity became a way to show my grandmother that I was part of her family and by taking her name, she would always be part of my family.

I had spent my childhood praying for

her salvation while she spent my childhood preparing to love me. I should have spent my childhood preparing myself to love her and she could
have spent my childhood praying for my salvation from my salvation.

I begin to work on developing this new
relationship with my grandmother.

After beginning the new relationship
with my grandmother I felt somewhat positive
about my parents and sisters. I had heard two
things that began to make me think about them
a lot.

The two things I heard were relatively
new concepts back then when I was 23. *Dialoguing* and *building bridges* sounded so noble
to me. It sounded like if I built a bridge to my
family and attempted to dialogue with them
about the gay issue that I could not appear to
have given up easily.

I wish I knew then what I know now
about those concepts. Nonetheless, I started
building a bridge to my family and attempted

to start dialogue with them.

Several weeks went by and I took a step back and examined what I was doing. I was building a bridge. But when I looked to the other side of the river, their side, there was no construction at all.

I started thinking about the dialogue. And, of course, I was the one doing all the dialogue. The traffic on the bridge was one way. It was always me to them.

I knew why. I knew it was because they really believed that they were right in their beliefs. I hated understanding that. I tried to think of one thing that I could bring up to them that would make them think about their beliefs like my homosexuality had made me think about mine. But there was nothing.

There was nothing except the sound of familial voices on the other end of the phone line repeating admonitions and biblical text, alleged Jesus quotes and the ultimate witnessing motivation, the pronouncements that they didn't want me to go to Hell.

I was very early in my coming out of fundamentalism process at this point. However, I had gained enough self-love and self-respect to know that I shouldn't ever let anyone tell me that I was going to Hell.

The more I thought about it, the more I realized that I had more respect for myself than to allow my family to abuse me like that. I would never allow a stranger on the street to tell me I was going to Hell, so why would I allow my family to do that?

I decided I needed to walk away. If my family at some point decided to come to me to talk about this subject, they could do so. And that's when the light bulb went on inside my head. I finally got what the dialoguing and bridge building were all about.

This was not about me making amends because I had not chosen religion over family.

And that's when I first felt peace about my decision to walk away. I knew my parents could never get to a place where they would compromise their hopes for eternity just to have a relationship with their son. They hadn't had a relationship with me at any point in my life anyway.

I knew when I walked away that there would never be a time that my parents could follow. Their decades of cultish fundamentalist Baptist Christianity had not only robbed them of the freedom and joy of living life, but it had also taken away their ability to love themselves, each other or their children.

It made perfect sense to me. But I decided that I couldn't let my parents abuse me out of pity for them and their lifestyle choice. So I walked.

I believe I chose to be gay in the same way
others choose to be straight.
I wish I didn't have to do the work that others
before me could have done.
I think any of us who have found it
should share it.
I'm afraid to lose my hair.
I know my sexuality is a big part of
who I am.

I believe parents should earn their children's
love and respect.
I wish I could show him how much
I love him.
I think he is beautiful.
I'm afraid my time will run out before enough
people have seen my light.
I know he loves me.

I was once told that I was lucky because I had experienced romantic love about five times in my my life.

Some were isolated, some were overlapping. Since getting older and somewhat wiser, I have realized the importance of those experiences and relationships in my own journey.

Someone you already know about...

Every passionate feeling, every standing of what I needed in my life. Shortly after moving to California and coming out to my family, I was walking to a frozen yogurt store near our apartment. A guy almost walked right into me. Our shoulders slammed together. I wasn't in pain but I turned around to see who it was.

He kept walking and then stopped in the parking lot about fifty feet away and leaned up against a car. That is when I saw his face. And that is when I recognized him.

It was Richard. He was one of the five people on my list of loves. He was the guy who cursed me after coming out to his family, thinking it would help our relationship only to find that I was already committed to being with Todd.

Every feeling I had ever felt toward him rushed up and down my spine at that moment.

I watched him as he lit up a cigarette. I could almost smell his brand in my nostrils. I knew exactly what that cigarette smelled like and I knew exactly what his lips would taste like after he smoked it.

I couldn't figure out what Richard was doing in California, especially since he had never told me anything about wanting to be there when we were together. For a moment, I wondered if he was there looking for me. It did seem like an enormous coincidence. But we didn't travel in the same circles back in Pennsylvania.

I quickly realized that if he was there to look for me, the only way he could have gotten my location was by going back to *Chi-Chi's* where I worked and where he left me. I had kept in touch with a couple of the waitresses there.

But that scenario seemed a little far fetched. I wasn't sure why he was there. I did know that I had a choice. I could walk over to him and start talking or I could just walk away and go home to Todd.

The urge to go and talk to him was unbelievably strong. I knew in my heart that if I went to talk to him that it would end up with me cheating on Todd. The feelings were that strong.

For a moment, I questioned why my feelings were still so strong for Richard. Wasn't being in a relationship supposed to kill all of those other feelings and desire? I couldn't believe I was thinking so sarcastically.

I knew myself well enough to know that my weakness for Richard was still there. I wasn't sure if I still loved him or if I was just horny and remembering that I still had never experienced sex like I had experienced with Richard.

I decided that if I needed to make my decision quickly since he was almost through with his cigarette.

So I walked away. I don't think I made a conscious decision to walk away. I just did it.

I figured I was preserving my relationship with Todd. Sex with Richard could never be casual or without deep feeling for me.

As I walked back to our apartment, I wondered what would have happened if I had taken the opposite action. I would never really know.

Someone you didn't know about but should...

The first time I saw this guy, he drove

right in front of me in his little blue car. He turned and looked up at me and smiled. It was the most beautiful smile I had ever seen. He had beautiful teeth and deep, brown eyes and a face that would make even the hardest of hearts swoon.

I thought I had already experienced all of the possible feelings associated with love. Somewhere in my life I had decided that there was nothing new I could feel when I looked at another guy. Somewhere in my life I had deceived myself because this guy was really doing a number on me.

At first, I thought I could grade what I felt as lust. I certainly did have that burning feeling inside my gut that I had felt many times before. The difference this time was the feeling inside went way beyond a sexual desire. But I wasn't sure how it could be more than just a sexual thing.

At that moment in my life, I wasn't in a place to think about being in love with this guy. So, I convinced myself and my pounding heart that I was mistaken.

When I kissed his lips, I told my heart that what I was feeling was a lie. When I touched his skin, I blocked the sensation of his warmth from my brain. When I explored his being, I convinced my own body that my reaction was just a momentary thrill. When it was over and he walked away from me, I listened to my own reasoning and closed the door to my heart.

Two days later, I was still reeling from the impact of his eyes and the taste of his kiss. I found myself constantly thinking about him. I could hear his voice, the way he said certain words and how he looked at me during that most important moment when we were together.

I found myself literally shaking my head back and forth trying to throw out the idea that this was more than that momentary thrill.

I picked up the phone and hesitantly dialed his number. What was I doing? I thought to myself. My heart was in no condition to let another love inside. Was it?

"Hi, it's me," I said, slowly. I wondered if he would even remember. It was completely plausible that I was alone in my swooning.

"I was hoping that you would call or email me," he said.

That one sentence was like sugar in my bloodstream. What was I doing, I questioned myself again. How could I sustain these feelings?

"I was wondering if you would like to get together again," I asked.

"Yeah, I would really like that," he replied.

More sugar.

"I really enjoyed the other night," I started. "Especially talking to you. That doesn't usually happen too much in these situations."

I could hear his muffled laughter. "You are right, it doesn't happen very often."

"When can you come over?" I asked, rather bluntly.

Two hours later I opened the door and there he was. And there *it* was. That feeling. The swooning. I looked right into his beautiful eyes and thought I saw what I had only seen in a few others. I thought I saw a completion of myself.

As we sat on the couch together I tried not to stare. After all, I didn't really know him very well and I certainly didn't want to overwhelm him. But there was just something about him. Something, again, that went beyond the burning inside. Then it happened again.

We sat for about thirty minutes and just talked. I found myself wanting to ask him personal questions. I held back considerably. I just listened to him speak and watched his beautiful face as we shared important insignificant details about our lives.

After I couldn't take anymore, I leaned over and kissed him right on the lips. I can only describe the feeling of his lips on mine as what I would suspect kissing an angel would be like. I know that sounds hopelessly cheesy but I was falling for him.

Within moments, I was taken to a place I had only been a few times in my life. I was not prepared to feel an even stronger passion than I had felt the first time we were together. I closed my eyes and rationalized my actions as final.

I lay next to him for about twenty minutes after our incredible experience. He lay on his back and I lay on my side looking at him. Fortunately, his eyes were closed so he was unaware of my stare.

Everything about him was so perfect from the profile of his face, the texture of his hair to the shape of his ears. I found myself captivated with every detail of his body. In the middle of my fascination, however, my heart kept skipping beats. I knew that falling for someone else was not in my life's plan.

I had already experienced love and there wasn't supposed to be any freedom, patience or desire to search for more. I had already wept tears for unrequited love a few times in my life and I wasn't interested in revisiting that pain. But here was a guy who was making me want to throw away everything I had ever thought or felt about love and my life.

This guy was changing me. He was making me want to change things about my life I would have never even considered changing.

Then, he looked at me and I fell for him.

There I was, sitting across the table from this guy in a pizza place. I knew he was thinking I was cheap by taking him there.

I suppose sometimes I was obvious in my observations of him. I suppose I wanted him to notice. No, I knew I wanted him to notice.

Whenever he looked at me I swooned. Here was a guy who was turning my world upside down. After just a couple weeks of seeing him off and on, I was ready to throw in the towel and find out why we weren't talking about what flowers to plant in our garden and what type of puppy to get. I guess in the back of my mind I knew the answer. I didn't want to think about that because it was too confusing, too challenging. So, I settled for sitting next to him and looking at him with adoration.

Most of our conversations were small talk but never cold or impersonal. There was a little distance in his eyes when I would try to ask questions that were too personal. He's protecting himself, I always thought to myself. Someone must have hurt him, I was sure of it.

One evening, as we walked once again to the cheesy pizza place, he opened up a little and shared some of his personal history which was a little like my own. Nothing too deep, just an acknowledgment that we had shared some of the same pain in our youth. For the first time I felt protective of him. I felt the urge to right every wrong in his life. I wanted to go back in time and soothe him after every heartache he had ever experienced.

As I tried to sleep that night I tried to kick every amorous thought toward him out of my head. I could not fall in love with someone I barely knew. I could not fall in love with some-one when

I was not in a place to love back if he fell for me. As much as I tried, I could not empty my head or my heart of the feelings inside.

I decided the next time that I saw him would be the last time. The situation was creating too much turmoil in my heart. The last five hours we spent together were hazy for me. I spent most of the time trying to shut the door to my heart. I tried not to look at the beauty of his face. I thought of someone else when I kissed his lips. And when it was over, I turned my head so I wouldn't see what I could be holding for the rest of my life.

I walked him to his car and kissed him goodbye. I made promises to write him emails and maintain a friendship. I made myself think away the urge to cry. I had not felt emptiness in my heart for ten years. But that night, as I watched his little blue car drive away from me, I realized there was still room in my heart.

Then, I went on with my life. Over the next four months I thought a lot about what I had discovered about myself and my own heart. I realized that not only had I learned something about myself and about love but I had discovered someone who was discovering the same thing. I suddenly realized that I had to make sure I didn't lose touch with this guy who was changing my life.

I tried my best to see him in December but I never even got close to his city. I emailed him and told him it might be January. When those plans didn't gel because of my work it seemed that maybe we wouldn't be able to see each other again very soon.

He also told me that he had started dating someone. I was somewhat frustrated at myself for not being more aggressive about pursuing him. But I was also happy for him. By the tone of his emails it didn't seem like the relationship was very serious but I panicked a little anyway.

Sometime in March, I don't remember what day, I asked him to just come to visit me. I hoped he could take some time off his work to come and see me. As fate would have it, he was no longer in the relationship he had told me about.

Within two weeks I was at the airport waiting for his plane.

I felt nervous, somewhat silly and so overwhelmed about what I might discover. After all, it had been seven months since I had even seen him. As I waited at gate N-7, I decided that I would accept whatever feelings I felt for him as soon as I saw him. Knowing myself, I knew I would be able to tell right away whether or not there would be something to talk about besides the weather.

He was one of the last people off the plane. I saw him several moments before he saw me. There he was. It was seven months later and this beautiful guy was walking toward me.

My heart was swimming around in my torso and then started pounding in my ears. He was amazing. His face, his eyes, his hair. Everything was beautiful. Even the bag over his shoulder was just right.

When he looked up at me he smiled the same smile as when we first met outside my hotel seven months earlier.

He stood in front of me as we rode the escalator to the baggage claim area. I felt myself swooning again. I gripped the handrail tightly as I tried to get control of my own emotions.

What was it about this guy that sent me over the edge every damn time I saw him? What about him made me want to walk away from everything in the life I knew just to be next to him? I usually had such control over my feelings.

We went from the airport to get something to eat. I still am not sure if it is improper to take your out-of-town guests to your favorite restaurant the first night they are in town but that's what happened. At least it was much better than the cheap pizza place. I sat across from him in the restaurant and wondered how this could be happening. Fortunately, our waitress, Brandy, knew what my regular order would be so I didn't have to think too much about my food.

The guy I had been thinking about for seven months was sitting across the table from me. All of the questions I had thought of over seven months, disappeared from my mind. I thought I was ready to ask him deep, probing questions about his feelings for me but I was so overwhelmed by my own feelings that I couldn't think about asking him anything.

"Did you ever think we would get around to seeing each other again?" I asked out of desperation. That was one of my questions but it was from the bottom of the list.

He looked at me and smiled.

God, those teeth and those lips.

"I hoped I would see you again but after all of your canceled trips I did begin to wonder."

"I know," I mumbled. "I'm sorry. These last seven months have been a mess. So many things going on with my work. It has been difficult to remember what state I am in let alone make time for a few days off."

"But I am here now," he said looking at me, still smiling.

"Yes," I smiled back. "And we are going to have fun this weekend. Our time will be filled with fun things."

"I hope so," he said, raising his eyebrows a little.

Later that night as he slept beside me, I realized that I had never had someone other than a boyfriend sleep overnight with me in my bed. At first, I was uncomfortable. I had always guarded my bed space. I sat up in my bed and looked over at him. His mouth was slightly open and he was making whimpering, puppy-like noises.

This time, the swooning in my heart was deeper. For the first time I felt more than love for him. This time, I felt I would be incomplete without him sleeping there. I had never even thought about having someone sleep on my right side. But there he was, changing my heart as he changed my life.

The hours flew by that weekend and I played host and he played tourist. Everything seemed so comfortable. For someone I didn't know very well, we certainly had an ease of sharing. Although, truthfully, for me the best part of the time we spent together was the time we lay together in bed and began to learn how to make love to each other.

The same passion and ecstasy that we shared seven months earlier was still there although a bit different. Maybe it was the openness of my heart and maybe the openness of his heart as well.

It didn't really matter to me. All I cared

about that weekend were the moments we were sharing right then.

Unfortunately, I spent most of Saturday evening in extreme pain from a migraine. I feared that he would just go explore the nightlife of the city with out me. Instead, he sat on my couch with my head in his lap and rubbed my temples and tried to ease my pain. As much pain as I was in, I was still able to see the significance in his expression.

As the hours ticked away and as the time of the flight that would take him away from me drew closer, anxiety kicked in. The thought of saying goodbye without a plan to see each other again before another seven months flew by was filling me with dread.

On Sunday morning, I awoke to find myself spooning him. As I kissed his ear, he woke up and turned his head to kiss me back.

"I can't believe that you are leaving today," I whispered into his ear. "This has been incredible."

"It has been really nice," he whispered back.

I wanted to ask him to never leave the bed. I wanted to find a way to make sure that he woke up in my arms every morning. But I couldn't find the words.

Later that day at the airport, I grabbed his hand as soon as they announced his flight was boarding. He took a step toward me and kissed me. I hugged him.

"I wish I wasn't going," he said in my ear.

I was so stunned I didn't know what to say. I wanted to pull him back to me so that he couldn't go. But then I wondered if he was joking. I couldn't tell. I could tell that my heart was sinking. As I watched him walk toward the gate, I felt that same swooning feeling but for the first time I felt something different.

I was sure that I was feeling love.

And that's why you should know about him.

I believe sensitive honesty is better than
protective lying.
I wish I didn't have to relive my past.
I think he knows I am the one.
I'm afraid my passion is passion.
I know many who share my history will never
be free.

I believe the guy I hold in my arms at night
needs me.
I wish my dogs would live forever.
I think if God wrote a book
it wouldn't be vague.
I'm afraid I'll find the truth before I am
finished searching for it.
I know love is the answer.

Part Four

I have reached an astounding realization as I am writing. I never knew my parents. (I still don't know them.) Of course, I knew their faces, parts of their personalities and their names but that is it. I still don't know who they are.

That is one of the most obvious revealing signs of someone who has successfully died to themselves.

A few years ago, my parents sold the home that I grew up in. I knew they were selling it. Not because they told me but because I had gone by the house when I was on a trip passing through that part of the state.

That visit was the first return to my home town since coming out to my biological family. Seeing a *for sale* sign on the house was a little stunning.

So much of my life had happened inside those walls. And with my parents selling that house, it felt to me that I would finally be able to move past everything in my history that was tied to 41 Shaver Avenue.

I also thought about the things inside that house that still belonged to me. There were several boxes holding things of my life that I had not taken with me when I left. I had a few choices. I could use the hidden key and go into the house and retrieve them. I could wait and just contact my parents and ask for my things. Or, I could walk away and let my past be my past.

I walked away. I had traveled too far forward in my journey to risk taking steps backward. It had been almost five years to the day since I had walked away from the spiritual terrorism and religious bigotry of my biological family. I knew I made the right decision once again because of the peace I felt in my heart.

A month or so later, my grandmother called me. There was a strange hesitancy in her voice.

"I have to tell you," she said slowly, "Your folks are selling the house and mentioned to me that there are some things of yours in the attic."

Why weren't they calling *me*, I wondered.

"Your mother asked me to call you and ask if you wanted your things," she continued.

I had to think about it for a minute. I was struggling with the concept that my own parents couldn't call me directly but had to use my grandmother to relay a message.

I did want my things. But then I thought of my let-my-past-be-the-past bravado from a few months earlier. I guess I felt stronger than I had when I was standing in front of my parent's house.

"I would like them."

"Ok, your mother offered to ship the boxes to me and then I will ship them to you. She just wanted money to cover the postage."

I couldn't believe that my mother wouldn't just ask for my address and send the boxes directly. I kept waiting for my grandmother to tell me that my parents asked her to ask me to call them. But it didn't happen.

I sent the money to my grandmother. About a month later, I got the boxes from my grandmother. I wondered if there would be note with my parent's new address or at least telephone number. But there was nothing.

My biological mother and father had moved and chosen not to tell me where their new home was. I felt uncomfortable not knowing. But I knew that it was a statement from them. More than anything else, it was a statement of their continued commitment to their faith. As twisted as I saw that to be, I understood what they were thinking. After all, I too, had once been the kind of person they were.

It always seemed to me that I was destined to be tied to the religion of my family in some way. I now know the reasons why but it wasn't always so apparent.

I think the second most-asked question to me is regarding my spirituality and religion at the present time. I know everyone is looking for their own answers but so many who have shared my journey are looking for guidance or at least a push in the right direction.

I have never wanted to be a preacher or a theologian. I still never want to be one which means that I also never pretend to be one. I will always leave that up to those who feel that is their importance in life.

However, I have had a journey which continues to this day.

After coming out to my family, I pretty much shed a lot of the ritual part of my religious beliefs and spirituality. In fact, I usually only went to church for special events, mostly tied to concerts.

My absence from regular church atten-dance had very little to do with the fact that I was gay and felt oppressed in some way by ev-ery church I had ever attended. For the most part, I was simply taking a step back and re-examining my beliefs and questioning a lot of what I had been taught was truth and what I had been taught about how to treat other people, women, minorities, etc.

I had gained a lot in my life through mu-sic. Some of the more contemporary and not so religious music by religious musicians still held something for me at that time.

One Saturday evening, Todd and I went to a concert by Margaret Becker to be held at one of the Calvary Chapel franchises in south-ern California. Since the tickets from TicketMaster that we purchased were general admission, we got to the church early so that we could get decent seats in the auditorium.

After a couple hours of waiting outside,

the doors to the auditorium were opened. To my confusion, the youth minister of the church was escorting attendees to specific seats.

When it came time for us to be seated, we were seated far from the fully vacant front seats. I later learned those were reserved for church members so that they would not have to wait outside. In addition to our "assigned"seats by the youth minister, we were also seated right behind a large support pillar for the ceiling of the auditorium. It was so large that we couldn't even see the stage.

To resolve the problem, we just scooted down to the end of the row of seats. The youth minister ran over in a tizzy and told us we would have to sit in the seats he had sat us in.

"But we can't see because of the support pillar," I explained.

"You can hear the music which is more important than seeing," he retorted rather crassly.

"Is the minister of the church here?" I

asked. "I would like to talk to him."

After a few minutes of searching, the youth minister brought the church pastor to our row of seats. I explained to him our situation and the youth minister's inability to resolve our problem.

The minister looked right into my eyes. "If you don't want to sit where we sat you then you should leave," he said without blinking.

"Are you serious?" I asked incredulously.

"Absolutely. Right there is the door."

I stood up at looked at him, searching for some trace of humanity.

"I have never been to this church before," I began. "You have no idea whether or not I am a Christian. I may be here tonight because I feel lost and am looking for spiritual answers. And you are telling me that if I don't sit in a specific seat that I have to leave?"

"That's right," he replied quickly. "There is the door."

It didn't take long for me to walk the few

steps to the door. Throughout the forty-five minute drive back to our apartment, I said a lot of words I was never allowed to say when I was a student at Jerry Falwell's university. But, I also swore to Todd that I would never step inside a church again for as long as I lived.

I was livid. I couldn't believe that I had given people involved with religion so many chances to trample on me. But I decided that would be the last time. It wasn't just that incident. It was the culmination of every incident like that which I had endured over the years.

I was probably more impatient than most since I was a preacher's kid and saw so many of the things in the back side of churches to which regular lay people remain unexposed. But the "Margaret Becker Incident" was the last straw for me. I was tired and needed a break. Besides, I was only lying to myself by thinking that I could honestly examine my beliefs and still be tied to the church in some way. So I walked.

At first I felt very unstable. My entire

life I had always felt that I would at least be able find some social structure and support within the church. Of course, the more I examined everything; I realized that, once again, I was kidding myself. The churches I had attended had never been a source of support to me. I had spent most of my Sundays trying church after church in my attempt to find that place of solace and peace everyone bragged that they offered.

During the early days of my coming out and beginning days of self-acceptance I had come to understand that I had a negative personal attribute of trying to do things to gain acceptance from other people. When I came out I realized I didn't need the acceptance of my family or friends.

When I started coming out of fundamentalist Baptist Christianity after the "Margaret Becker Incident," I realized that I had still been seeking the acceptance of my religion. I knew I had to work more on self acceptance and discard that persistent need for acceptance by others. Regardless of whether or not God existed or thought homosexuality was right or wrong, I was gay and happy to be part of that family of people.

I began my process by attempting to empty from my head the years of brainwashing. I had fundamentalist Baptist Christian doctrine pumping through my veins and into my heart.

Not long after I came out to my family, I was hired by a $300 million financial services company in Los Angeles. My position required me to assist the Marketing Director in developing marketing plans, designing brochures and other collateral pieces to make services more understandable and accessible to their clients.

My boss was a woman which worked well as I always seemed to work better with a female boss. Liza reported directly to the CEO of the company which also meant I had a great deal of interaction with him as well.

I was working at this company for about two weeks when the CEO, Nathan Rifcke, came into my secluded cubicle.

"I just wanted to tell you," he said, sitting on the edge of my desk, "that you are doing a great job. I have heard great reports from Liza about the improvements you are making to our marketing materials."

"Thanks," I replied. "I am really enjoying being here. It's a little different from my last position but I like the challenge."

He was the CEO so I was digging deep for all the corporate mumbo jumbo I could find. Since this was my first corporate job, I knew I wasn't digging deep enough.

"I think you are a great addition to our staff," he continued. "I want you to feel totally comfortable coming and talking to me about anything."

That sounded weird to me since I was

supposed to share my ideas first with my boss. But I nodded and smiled in agreement. I was flattered that he was at least noticing my work and impressed by the little I had done over the first two weeks.

After that first conversation, I started to notice that Mr. Rifcke seemed to come into my cubicle every day and compliment me on my work. I assumed that I must be doing a knock-out job of schmoozing by all of his attention.

About one month into my employment, I was in the copy room making some copies of pie charts and I felt someone walk up beside me and put their arm across my shoulder. I have never been used to strangers touching me so I jumped a bit.

I turned to see Mr. Rifcke standing next to me smiling. I was startled and a little uncomfortable but I didn't shy away too much. He didn't say a word. He just stood there for a moment, smiling at me. Then he turned around and walked away.

It did seem a little strange that he was taking so much interest in me but I dismissed it.

Four months later I was sitting at my desk and was surprised by Mr. Rifcke's hands on my shoulders. This time he proceeded to give me a backrub.

My first thought was that he was wrinkling my nicely pressed white shirt. (Another confirmation of my hardwired homosexuality.) My second thought was that it actually felt good. I had been sitting at my computer for a couple hours working on a new marketing campaign.

"I think you and I should go out to dinner sometime," he said softly.

I was glad that he couldn't see my face. It was at that exact moment that it dawned on me that he was coming on to me. I always prided myself in my gaydar but he had fooled me. I had never even once thought about him being gay.

Maybe it was because he wasn't attractive to me. I don't know. I do know that it took a little work for me to escape from the dinner invitation diplomatically.

A few hours later I felt strange about being so concerned about not offending him. He was stepping way over the boundaries of any boss/employee relationship. For one fleeting moment, I thought about the money I might be able to get from a sexual harassment suit against my employer.

But, the more I thought about it, the more I became bored with the idea. So I dismissed it from my mind. I tried to avoid him as much as possible. I didn't think he noticed my discomfort and I didn't want to talk about it. I didn't want to jeopardize my own personal peace at my job.

A few years later I realized that I should have taken different action in the entire matter. Once again, the issue of my homosexuality came into play.

I quit my job at that $300 million financial services company in 1993. I really felt I needed to focus on completing and publishing *The Preacher's Son* and Todd and I were financially sound. It was also an excuse for me to leave a company where I no longer felt welcome.

Over time, I felt that my creativity was being stifled and the money that I was saving the company was no longer important to my boss. I wanted to work somewhere that I was respected and made to feel like a valuable member of a team.

I finished *The Preacher's Son* and began shopping around for a publisher. It was a time consuming process. I sent dozens of query letters to mainstream as well as gay publishers.

The mainstream publishers kept pushing for a Kitty Kelly type book about Jerry Falwell. Everyone was interested in dirt about the one televangelist who had not had a major public scandal in his ministry.

The offer was very tempting. I had seen and heard enough during my time in Lynchburg to write some juicy material. Not nearly as scandalous as Jim and Tammy Bakker or Jimmy Swaggert, however, it would definitely feed a certain audience's hunger for anything against someone they mistakenly thought was doing everything he did for money and power.

As I contemplated the offer, I remembered everything I had given up to find freedom. I also remembered how difficult it had been to write *The Preacher's Son*. I also remembered my friends who were forever gone from me.

The result of my decision is *The Preacher's Son* as it was published. I've never regretted giving up money and power to stay true to my intentions.

After I made all of those important decisions about *The Preacher's Son*, I decided to give the corporate world another shot. I accepted a job offer from a $33 million company in West Los Angeles. It was a much smaller company than the financial services company but it was a better position.

As the advertising manager, I had my

creative plate filled everyday. I had a great office and a $3 million budget at my creative disposal to design and create incredible advertising and marketing materials.

I decided when I started this job that I would not be in the closet. I really didn't hesitate to tell the truth about myself and my life. At first, the Monday morning weekend review discussions in the lunch room always ended up with me exiting before it was my turn to talk. After a couple months, I was ready to tell the truth.

For some reason I knew the day that it would happen.

"Hey Marc, I never noticed that ring on your finger before."

Leave it to Leticia to notice my jewelry. She was pointing out the ring on my right ring finger.

"Are you married?" she asked, as a small crowd gathered. Apparently, everyone in the company was waiting for this moment.

"I am."

"Oh, I didn't know that," she replied. "What's her name?"

"*His* name is Todd," I said.

I could see a few shadowy figures move from the crowd and leave the lunch room. But the remaining group seemed to crowd in closer to me. It was as if I had just revealed that I had a third arm and everyone wanted to make sure they got a good view.

"So," Leticia continued, "Tell us about him. You know there haven't been very many gay people to work in this company. At least anyone who was out. Why do you wear your ring on your right hand?"

"I wear it on my right hand because straight people wear their wedding rings on their left hand. I don't want anyone to mistake me or my relationship as a straight."

It was then that I realized that maybe I could do something good for myself and any other gay person who might walk in the doors of that company. So I spent a few moments talking and sharing a brief introduction of my real self and Todd.

An hour later, I was sitting in my office when Dani, the Human Resources Manager stopped in front of my door.

"I didn't know you were gay," she whispered with her head in my office doorway.

"Until today, I didn't realize that everyone assumed I was straight," I said boldly.

She just smiled and walked into her office and closed the door. Her office was right next to mine and we shared a common wall. Even if she closed her door, I could hear every word of every conversation. And that day, as soon as she closed her door, I could hear her excited conversation with one of the vice presidents. It made me feel a little weird. But I shrugged it off as heterosexual hysterics.

My comfort level with being out at work grew rapidly over the ensuing months. I felt more empowered to speak up for myself and others like me. It was something I never thought

I would be able to do.

December 1 came and right outside my office window at the intersection of Veteran and Wilshire, a large group of people had gathered to protest the government's lack of concern over HIV research and funding. The most dramatic moment was when the activists carried a large wooden coffin to the middle of the intersection and set it on first.

It was pretty much pandemonium. My office window had a great view of the activities. One of the sales reps for our company came in to my office to watch was what happening. His name was Greg. I didn't know him too well, but I knew that he was not the most comfortable with me being gay.

"So, why aren't you down there, Marc?" he asked, breaking a silence.

That was the last question I expected to be asked. And it made me wonder. *Why wasn't I down there?*

"That's a good question," I admitted. "I

didn't know something like this would be going on today. Why aren't you down there?"

I felt pretty smug with my own question.

"I've never been someone who has gotten involved in causes," he replied. "Don't you think that those people could get more attention for their cause if they weren't so radical? To people like me, seeing them cause this commotion doesn't make me feel anything for their message. It just makes me aggravated that traffic will be a mess when I leave for home."

"I'm not so sure that this is really about winning people over to their side," I said, slowly. "I think it more about making a public statement about what is happening or in this case what's not happening."

"Don't you think that this is too aggressive?" he asked. "Do you really want to turn off non-gay people who actually might be allies?"

"Tell me this, Greg. What if your wife had breast cancer? What if you knew that our country could be doing more to help save her life and the multitudes of other men and women who suffer from breast cancer? What if you knew your wife died because our country was dragging their feet with research and treatment options. How angry would that make you? To what extent would you go to make sure that your wife's voice was heard?"

Greg actually turned red. "I would do everything I could no matter what it cost me. I guess it would be the ultimate display of love for my wife."

I smiled. "That's probably how you should think about these people down here. They are making statements for themselves, for their husbands, their wives, their boyfriends, their sons and daughters and their friends. I think its okay to get mad about things that are truly horrific. I think history will one day mourn that our country and others were too prudent in their response and in research."

"Wait a minute," Greg interrupted. "Did

you say something about men having breast cancer?"

"Yeah, I did. Most people don't think about it. But it happens. More often than you think."

Greg nodded. "Okay, you've given me a while bunch of stuff to think about and find out about. I'm going back to my desk."

I sat down in my chair as he left. I felt proud of myself. I got back up and looked at the people demonstrating outside. I hoped I had done something that they needed me to do.

A few months later, Dani was in her office with the door open. She was on the telephone with the controller in the accounting department. I could tell by the tone of her voice that the conversation was not going well.

I heard her slam the receiver down against the telephone.

"That fucking faggot!" she yelled.

I was frozen in my chair. I suddenly felt

unsafe in a company in which I was just getting comfortable. To top it off, the controller wasn't even gay.

I noticed over the ensuing months that Dani had a lot of people problems. Once when she was escorting a black male applicant into her office for an interview, she stopped just outside my door and looked up at him.

"You are so tall!" she said. "I bet you play a lot of basketball."

He looked into my office and we caught each other's eye. I hoped he could see in my eyes that I was telling him that she was a crazy person and he should run out of the building and never look back.

One of my responsibilities was to oversee the company booth at several industry-related conferences in southern California. The largest conference was in Long Beach and the first year I had to set up everything, I brought along one of the other male workers to help with assembly etc. It was a huge job and Jerome was happy to get out of the accounting office for a day to help.

I had only had very brief interactions with Jerome during the time I had been at the company. He was always friendly.

As we were driving the company van to Long Beach to set up, he popped the question.

"Are you gay?" he asked out of the blue.

"Ah, yes. I am."

Suddenly, he relaxed. "I thought you were but I wasn't sure. Do you know I'm gay?"

"Um, no." The thought had never crossed my mind.

Well, I am. My boyfriend and I have been together for 11 years."

"That's pretty nice," I replied.

"Yeah, it's nice. So what's your story?"

I gave him the run-down on my gay life and romances and flings. It was the first time I had told anyone else but Todd everything there was to know about my life. I felt good.

"So have you and Todd ever had a

threeway?"

I was stunned into silence. I didn't expect that question. I had never been asked that
question. Except by Todd three weeks into our
relationship. I was uncomfortable with the discussion in 1988 and I was still uncomfortable.

"Um, no," I replied. "Isn't that like cheating?"

"It depends on how you look at it. I think
cheating is when you do something behind
someone's back and you don't tell them. I'm
talking about a mutually shared experience with
someone else."

My head was spinning. I suddenly felt
threatened by the conversation. Everything that
I ever thought was real about my relationship
started coming into question. I glanced sideways
at him trying to figure out if he was going to ask
me to have a threeway with him and his boyfriend or more, ask if he could have a threeway
with me and my boyfriend. Too be honest, I
started feeling a little crazy.

"I'm only asking because my boyfriend and I have been going through some things and I need to talk to someone about it."

Suddenly, I felt relieved.

"What kind of things are you going through?"

Jerome sighed and paused a moment before he continued.

"Well, we've been together for a long time. I am pretty conservative. When we first got together I used to be very jealous if he even looked at another guy or if another guy looked at him."

"Same here," I injected.

"A couple of years ago, Gary asked me what I thought about having a more open relationship. My first reaction was that I didn't want to do it. I told him I could never do something like that. But, then, I started thinking about it. I thought about how much I loved Gary and how much he loved me. I tried to find a reason in my head and heart why we wouldn't do it."

"What about the reason that you don't want other guys touching your guy?" I said sarcastically.

"That was the big thing for sure. But I really started thinking about what I was afraid of. I came to realize that I was just afraid of losing him because some other guy was a better kisser or better in bed. And I also thought that while there were things we could share with other people, I really needed something to just be ours. Our sex together was something only we could see and share."

"I think I agree with all of that." I said. "But you know, I come from a horribly conservative upbringing so I think I might be a little behind in my thinking sometimes."

"Me too," Jerome admitted. "So, we did it. We picked someone we were both into and we tried it. Our promise to each other was that we would stop immediately if the other person felt uncomfortable in any way. We had hand signal codes and everything."

"Sounds like a lot of work for an orgasm," I said.

"It was awkward at first," Jerome admitted. "But Gary and I were so in tune with each other that we didn't have anything strange happen. It was a great experience."

Good for you, I thought.

"So that leads me to why I brought this all up," Jerome said, slowly.

"What?"

"A couple years ago, almost three years now, Gary and I met this guy named Ryan. When we first met up with him we had a really nice time together. But then after that, I couldn't stop thinking about him. I talked to Gary about it and he suggested something that we had heard of other people doing but had never even thought about for ourselves."

"What was that?"

"He asked me if I could ever be in a relationship where there were three people instead of two."

Suddenly, the drive to Long Beach seemed to be taking way to long. But traffic was moving at a snail's pace and I was stuck with the continuation of the conversation.

"What did you tell him?"

"I told him the truth. I told him that I had read some articles in *Frontiers* about polyamorous relationships and that I had thought about whether or not I could deal with something like that. I had already decided that I could try it."

"Don't you think it would be way too complicated? Not to mention what your mother would think?"

Jerome laughed. "Well, the truth is that it is only complicated sometimes. But not any more complicated than it was when there were only two of us. And my mother loves having yet another gay son."

Jerome's admission was not as startling to me as it would have been a day earlier. Suddenly, I was curious.

"How do people usually react when you tell them this?"

He shrugged. "I use some discretion when I tell people. Some people can't handle that I'm even gay. When I came out, I chose not to be closeted about my life. I guess I'm still in the closet about this to a lot of people but I really don't care. Who I love and who I sleep with is really just my own business. Other people's judgment really doesn't affect me anymore."

"I'm just starting to think that way."

I wasn't sure I could ever be in love with two people at the same time in the same way. Everything that Jerome told me on that drive to Long Beach, challenged me to examine my own prejudices and ideals.

The more I thought about the entire discussion, the more I realized that I was thinking about relationships the way that I had been trained to think about them.

I had taken the rules and ideals about relationships from my pseudo hetero days and was just applying to my real gay life.

I could still hear Jerry Falwell in church and chapel. "One man, one woman, one lifetime."

That's when I thought about how ridiculous it was for me or any other gay person to try to model our relationships after that model. I was gay and I was in a relationship with another man. It was very different from being in an opposite sex relationship. While I might have shared common domestic chores with my heterosexual friends, the emotional and sexual part of my relationship was very different.

The company reinstated an office decorating policy that allowed employees to put personal pictures on their desks. Since there were only five men out of sixty-five employees, this new policy only seemed to affect the girls who wanted to have pictures of their boyfriends plastered all over their cubicles.

The policy wasn't gender specific so I planted a nicely framed picture of Todd on my desk. It was by no means a defiant move, I simply wanted to see his picture and also let my co-workers see a little more of my life.

It wasn't on my desk for two hours before Dani, the HR manager spotted it. She didn't say anything but I knew she would soon be on her way to my boss, the CEO, to share the juicy news.

Working at that company was often reminiscent of growing up in my home as a kid. My four sisters always seemed to have a knack for not keeping their mouths shut. So anything I shared with one of them always seemed to make it around to all of them.

At this company, office gossip always spread fast. As the only out person there, I could tell that I was the subject of many hushed conversations. But I went on with my work.

One of my strong points in my marketing skills was getting thirty to forty percent returns on direct mail pieces. The accepted average return was ten percent. Another strength was my ability to produce exquisite pieces each year and save about $100,000 in production costs.

I struck up a work friendship with my boss' secretary, Linda. Initially, it began as a way for us to vent about the idiosyncrasies of the CEO. Eventually, I learned that this relationship gave me insight into what my boss thought about me. He always confided in his secretary and with a couple bagels, I seemed to be able to drain her of information quite easily.

I had just passed my three year anniversary mark with the company and was gloating over saving the company yet another $100,000 when I first realized that something was terribly wrong. I was sitting in Linda's office wasting time until my lunch break.

"Have you seen *Priscilla, Queen of the Desert* yet?" she asked.

"No," I said smiling. "Not yet." I thought it was amusing that she thought I must surely have seen the recently released gay movie.

"I am planning on a trip later this year so I am saving a lot of my money for that," I said.

"Well, once you get that $25,000 bonus, you won't have to worry about saving money."

"What $25,000?"

"You don't know about that?" she asked incredulously. "The company is giving each manager a $25,000 bonus this year. Weren't you at the meeting?"

As soon as she finished her sentence a weird expression crossed her face. I suppose she realized that she had just revealed a secret to the one manager who was not getting the $25,000.

I don't know how I managed to get out of her office. I was furious. All at once, everything started making sense to me. I had felt slighted on several occasions. I had brushed it aside as paranoia. But this confirmed many of my suspicions.

Todd and I talked about the situation. We weren't in a financial situation for me to just quit my job without something else waiting for me. So, I agreed to stick it out for a while longer. We also agreed that I should keep my eyes and ears open a little more. He also consulted with an employment attorney and she encouraged me to get evidence and information.

Suddenly, everything started becoming too complicated. I had just fought the battles with my family and I was bored by the thought of having to fight again. After a long talk with Todd, I decided to take action into my own hands. I wanted to hold all the power and not wield it away.

I continued to hear everything that went on in Dani's office. To this day, it is hard for me to believe that she had no clue how loud she was even with the door closed.

One Friday afternoon, I heard her talking on the telephone to the company attorney. I had heard her trivial discussions with the attorney many times. This one sounded different.

"We have made a decision to get rid of

Marc," she said very audibly.

I was stunned. Was I hearing right or was I hearing wrong words coming from behind her closed door.

"We decided that since he doesn't have a personality that we no longer want to have him as an employee," she continued.

No personality? That was the first time I had ever heard anyone say that about me. I always assumed I had a personality but apparently I had been mistaken.

"We want to get rid of him without him knowing that we are just getting rid of him."

There was a silence for a few moments.

"No, on his last review, he scored high, got a $5,000 raise and a promotion. There isn't anything wrong with his performance. But a couple months ago he did change his name."

I didn't need to listen to anything else. I knew what was happening. It was hard to believe that they would take the risk of firing me for being gay but I knew and they probably knew that the anti-gay discrimination laws in California didn't have any real teeth.

When she wrapped up that phone call she immediately called the *Los Angeles Times* classified advertising department and placed an ad for my position.

The plan was to hire someone before they fired me so that they could make a transition quickly and without any downtime in the department. She explained all of this on the phone to the salesperson at the *Times*. The same sales person I always dealt with when I placed ads for the company.

It was then, that I knew I would have to play hardball. This would be my opportunity to gain control of the situation and make sure that everything worked out to my benefit and not theirs.

I waited about ten minutes after Dani finished placing the ad for my position with the sales person at the *Times*. Then, I called the same sales person. I wanted to make her lie to me.

Marc Adams 100

"Karen!" I said enthusiastically when she answered. "It's Marc Adams."

"How are you?" she said very slowly.

"I'm doing great. Just so you know, there will not be any ads placed this weekend for any of the branch offices. I just need to know for budgetary purposes if anyone from the company is placing any other ads for personnel."

"No."

She said it so quickly it was as if she knew I was going to call her and put her in the corner.

"Okay," I replied. "Thanks."

On Sunday morning, there it was. It was a blind ad with replies and resumes to be sent to a *Times* mailbox. I could see Dani's ignorance of my job requirements in her ad. It was almost comical as I read what she thought I did for my job.

On Monday morning, I took that page of the classified ads and folded it with that ad showing and placed it on the corner of my desk in my office. Everyone who walked into my office could not help but see the paper.

It was my first step in taking control. I hoped upon hope that my boss or Dani would see that I had found the ad or at least become paranoid that their plan was becoming exposed.

Todd and I had a lot of discussions about what I needed to do next. During our travels in the previous year, we had discussed many times the option of moving and we both had agreed that if we did ever move from Los Angeles, Seattle would be the choice because of all the obvious benefits for gay people who live there.

I watched over the next week as Dani, tried to sneak applicants for my job past my office door and into her office. My position was the only creative position in the entire company. She was much diluted, thinking that I wouldn't catch on to all those interviewees walking into her office carrying huge portfolios of their creative work.

A week and a half after they started running the ad for my position, I walked into the owner's office. He had been my boss for almost four years and as I looked at him I felt so repulsed. Here was a man who was cutting me out of a $25,000 manager's bonus and was underhandedly getting rid of me in spite of the huge amounts of money I had saved the company.

I placed my letter of resignation on his desk in front of him.

"What's this?" he asked, still completely oblivious to what was in the letter.

"I will paraphrase it for you," I said quickly. "I have decided to move to Seattle. This letter gives you sixty days notice of my leaving. That also gives us time to find someone to take my position. If we can make the hire soon enough, I can even train the replacement."

At first, my boss looked at me with disbelief. In his tiny, turtle-like head, I was sure he was trying to figure out if this was good for him or not. In my spinning head, I knew it was good for me. I had successfully extended my time and my paycheck at the company for two months. There was no longer a need to fire me if I was quitting.

I knew I would have been let go within a week if I had not submitted that letter. This way I would get two months additional pay and I could be better prepared for the changes that would come about in our lives as a result of moving to Seattle.

As I left his office, I felt a huge weight fall off my shoulders. I really did want to move to Seattle. It had been on my mind since my first visit there a year earlier. Everything that had happened at my job just pushed us to make our decision.

After returning to my office I immediately heard Dani's phone ring and she ran out of her office into my boss' office. About a half an hour later, she emerged and walked right into my office.

I don't remember what I expected her to say or do but I didn't expect her to break out in hives.

"I just found out about your move to Seattle," she said, almost breathlessly.

"Yes, I am looking forward to being there."

Her eyes went from mine down to the newspaper on the corner of my desk.

"You know," she said, "You are leaving at the right time."

"Oh really?" I couldn't help but force some sarcasm in my delivery.

Our plan was to move to Seattle at the end of October, 1997. In early September, I started to receive some telephone calls and emails from various universities and other gay-related groups. I was being asked to come and speak.

I wasn't really into the idea of getting up in front of a group of strangers and talking about the things I shared in *The Preacher's Son*. But I started doing it anyway. I wanted to get the story out in people's hands and most of the people from these groups didn't want me to just come and sign books and leave.

So I faced my fear of public speaking and began scheduling presentations around the country.

After the second presentation, I realized that I wasn't feeling the panic and fear I assumed I would feel. It was actually very easy. So I started scheduling more and more presentations. My goal was to fill up an entire year of programs.

I noticed that the groups I was speaking to were very diverse in their purpose. Except one segment of the population.

The only churches that were asking me to speak were Unitarian Churches and Fellowships. I kept approaching gay and gay friendly churches but, with only two exceptions, I had the door closed in my face. Sometimes literally.

I couldn't figure it out. I had assumed that the other religious groups would be the most open to hearing about my journey since members of their congregation and leadership had experienced similar journeys.

I was on the phone with a program coordinator for a large chain of gay churches. As I explained my book and presentation, he cut me off.

"I don't think we would be interested," he said abruptly.

"Do you mind if I ask why?" I asked.

"Well, too much of what you are sharing in your story makes Christianity look too prejudiced against homosexuality. There are some members in our church who are not very familiar with that part of Christianity and I am not willing to be the one to expose them to it."

"I don't understand."

"Let me put it this way. If you were coming to preach a sermon with a gospel message without any mention of homosexuality, it would be okay. But I think you are going to expose the side of Christianity that we don't want to expose."

I got out the conversation as quickly as I could. In the ensuing days, I began asking more and more questions every time someone turned me down for a presentation. Again, the gay and gay friendly churches were at the top of the list of groups refusing to have me speak.

I did, however, begin to get more and more explanations for the refusals. One very large gay Christian church in Florida told me that because I had not been on *Oprah*, I would not be allowed to speak.

So I stopped asking and began focusing my energy on the groups that were glad to host me.

I didn't know very much about being a Unitarian. Growing up in the home and church environment that I did, I had a pretty warped education about other religions. I had been taught that Unitarians were mostly over aged hippies who sacrificed things in the mazes behind their churches.

One Sunday before speaking in my first

Unitarian Fellowship, I looked at a poster hanging in the lobby titled, *"What Unitarian Universalists Think About God."*

It was quite a lengthy explanation which included points of view from many different people's journeys. But all of a sudden, it hit me what being a Unitarian was all about.

As I looked around the sanctuary, I saw people from every possible age group, religious background, political background, and family type. The one thing that drew them all together every Sunday was not their common beliefs but their uncommon beliefs. Each person was there, without guilt, to further their own spiritual journey. Each person was there to respect and learn from other people's journeys.

The churches I had attended were always driven by sameness and conformity. Questions, clothing, and different ideals about spirituality were shunned. But I was finally in a place where all of that was welcome.

That realization changed my life. It allowed me to embark on a journey that will continue the rest of my life.

I discovered that being a Unitarian was not about sacrificing things in a maze behind the church. It was about being who you are, as you are without apology and without exclusion. That's where I finally found my peace.

"You know I worry about you," my grandmother said to me.

We were sitting in her small apartment in Harrisburg during one of our visits to see her.

"I get very upset every time I think about that poor boy in Wyoming. I know that with your work you travel in some places that could be dangerous."

"Yes," I admitted, "it could be dangerous but we are very careful and use our heads."

I wanted to know more about her though and the small talk we were having was not enough.

"Grandma, I want to know what things happened in your life that made you understand who I was."

She laughed and grabbed my hand.

"Marc, I could tell you some stories."

"I want to hear them!"

"Well, I grew up on a farm. Not every animal had nookie with another animal of the same sex. It was quite common."

So my Grandmother thinks there isn't much difference between me and my boyfriend and two horny homosexual sheep, I thought to myself.

"You know, when you were still living at home, I attended this one church for a while. I had many friends. One Sunday during the sermon, the minister stopped and pointed his finger right at one of my girlfriends and said, 'I know you are a lesbian, get out.' Marc, you wouldn't believe the look of shock and shame on my friend's face."

My grandmother stopped speaking for a good forty-five seconds trying to hold her composure.

"My friend stood up in the middle of that crowded church auditorium and had to walk all the way out. Not one person said anything to her and no one said anything about the minister doing that. I decided that since there were so many cowards in that church that I would be a true friend."

"What did you do?" I asked.

"I stood up and followed her out that door. I was the only person who went with her and I never darkened the door of that church again. They probably thought I was her girlfriend but I didn't care."

I was overwhelmed. My grandmother had been demonstrating true love before I had even come to understand who it was that I was.

"When I used to work at the nursing home, in the late eighties there were a couple of younger male patients who came in. They had

AIDS and they were dying. The other nurses on my shift didn't want to have anything to do with them. That just made me sick to my stomach."

I couldn't believe I was hearing this from my grandmother.

'So," she continued, "I was the one who bathed them and sat with them and did what I could to make them feel comfortable and cared for. And, because I did all of that, I got to see their families visit them. Or not visit them. I got to see the dynamics of their relationships with their men friends."

"Do my parents know that you did this?"

Grandma laughed again and squeezed my hand even harder.

"I've done alot of things your parents don't know about."

And then she just kept laughing. Even though I had no idea she had been doing those things when she did them, at that moment, I felt like she had done those things for me.

After that conversation, I understood even

On October 22, 2003, we went to see my Grandmother in Harrisburg. It was one of our typical trips. Whenever I would be traveling in that part of the country we made a concentrated effort to go through Harrisburg and see her. We got to see her about two or three times each year which all of us anticipated each year.

This most recent trip went pretty much like the others. We met up at her apartment and then we drove in her car to eat dinner. Riding in my Grandma's car while she was driving was always an adventure. She was 86 years old and didn't have any physical problems except for some hearing difficulty. Her driving ability was pretty good if there was no one else on the road. We always found it amusing that she would complain about bad drivers while she was driving on the opposite side of the road.

Each dinner was the same in that she took us to Old Country Buffet. Each trip to see her and each trip to this restaurant became a tradition for us. Besides the company and conversation, I think her favorite part was sending us up to the ice cream machine to make her a sundae. She would always say that she only wanted a very small amount of plain ice cream. When we would return with an parlor-style ice cream sundae, her face would light up and she would wink at us.

After dinner, we would always go back to her apartment and talk. She was the reigning Skipbo and Jenga queen and so we would always have to play a few rounds of each game. It was embarrassing because we would always lose and she would always win.

On this most recent trip I felt some pangs of sadness as I watched her deal the cards. Her hands looked very old to me and were covered with age spots and bruise marks. She had mentioned that she seemed to be bruising very easy whenever she would bump into things.

I could remember very clearly when her hands did not look so old and her fingers were straight and without any arthritis in her finger joints. As I looked up at her, our eyes met. It was almost like she knew what I was thinking. Her eyes got watery and she reached across the table and squeezed my hand very briefly.

When it was time to leave, she kissed me on the lips and hugged me.

"I love you so much," she said.

I could feel her clinging to me. I felt her jerk a little and I realized that she was crying.

"Grandma loves you, always remember that," she said.

"I love you too," I replied. "We will see you in a couple months."

She just looked at me with tears in her eyes and hugged me again.

It was always tough to say goodbye to her when the visit was over. But we managed and we returned to our work on the road.

A couple months later we sent her our usual Christmas gift of special flavors of tea bags. We also found a great flower kit at Target which included a pot, planting soil and a tulip bulb. I bought it for her because I knew how frustrated she had been over the recent years that she could no longer grow her flower garden because of her arthritis.

She was elated with her tea and the flower kit. We were happy that we had made her happy with something unexpected.

Each year for about eight years now, I have made presentations at Eastern Washington University in Spokane, Washington. Typically, I do these programs in January. January, 2004, was no exception. The only difference is that I was able to schedule an additional presentation at Washington State University about 90 miles away during the Spokane trip.

On January 22, we drove from Eastern Washington University to Washington State University to do the second presentation. Just as we were driving into Pullman, Washington, our cell phone rang.

"Hi, this is Marc," I answered.

"Hi Marc, this is Cindy. Do you remember me?"

I knew exactly who she was. It was my Grandmother's stepdaughter. We had just met with Cindy during one of the recent trips to see Grandma. I then knew why she was calling.

"Yes, I do."

"I have some bad news. Your Grandmother has pneumonia and she is in the hospital. She went in last night. And it doesn't look good. She is on the highest level of antibiotics they have but she isn't responding to them. Her lungs are filling up with fluid and they are pumping them regularly."

My heart began sinking in my chest. Suddenly, my head was filled with every conversation I had ever had with my Grandma about her wishes when this day came.

"They put her on a ventilator," Cindy said. "Even though her living will has a do not resuscitate order in it. It doesn't look very good for her. Her kidneys are failing also and her heart is not working right. They put feeding tubes into her stomach."

Only one thing seemed important to me at that moment. I knew my Grandmother, for whatever reasons, had designated my father as the decision-maker for this moment. But I also knew that my mother's disdain for my Grandma would really come through. I also knew she did not ever want to be on a ventilator or have feeding tubes into her stomach.

"What's the point of having a living will if the hospital won't follow it?" I asked.

"I think the hospital called your father and he said to keep her on the ventilator for a while to see if she responds."

"So are my parents there with her?"

"No, Cindy replied, "they are not there. We've been trying to get them to go but your mother doesn't feel like they need to go and there's some discussion about your father not feeling well."

Within seconds, years of peace from my separation from my parents just disappeared.

What Cindy had told me was typical activity. Proving that my parents were incapable or unwilling to examine their lives.

"Do I need to come?"

"Well, it is up to you, Marc. She is pretty much out of it. She didn't really recognize me today. I am not sure that she would recognize you. She can't have any flowers in critical care but she can have cards."

"Okay, the first thing we will do is send a card. I will need you to let me know about how she is doing. I really don't have anyone in my immediate family who will be telling me anything."

"I know that."

My fear was almost overwhelming. I always knew that I would one day get this kind of news. I guess I just didn't expect it to be so soon. After all, there hadn't been a death in my immediate biological family in almost 16 years. And now, the one person who meant something to me was slipping away.

By the end of that week, I learned from Cindy that my parents still had not shown up to visit my grandmother in the hospital. I started feeling the same anger I had felt every day of my life as a child. It was a strange feeling. I found out through Cindy that two of my sisters had been to visit my Grandmother but had been encouraged by my mother not to do so.

I realized that forgiveness had been over-rated for me. My parents were exactly the same people. Twelve years had not made any difference in their lives. Then it hit me, I had forgiven people who had not asked for forgiveness.

The afternoon that I came to that realization was monumental to me. Even though my Grandmother was dying in a hospital two thousand miles away from me, she was still teaching me things.

On Sunday evening, January 31, I got the call that they had finally taken my Grandmother off of the ventilator and were ready to implement her wishes. The right side of her heart had stopped functioning along with her kidneys. I sat at my computer that night, all night, just waiting for the telephone to ring. My boyfriend and I began to mourn deeply as time passed. I knew it would soon be over. There would be no more Jenga, no more Skipbo, no more Old Country Buffet sundaes and no more driving on the opposite side of the street.

I began to think about how much I needed my Grandmother. I had never allowed myself to need anyone in my biological family because I knew they could never be there for me. Over the twelve years I had spent getting to know my Grandmother, I had torn down the walls and allowed myself to need her. I needed one person in my biological family to tell me they loved me and mean it. I needed one person in that family to say Merry Christmas and Happy Birthday. I needed to not be without the one person who had taught me so much about life and love and kindness.

A few hours into February 2, I got the

phone call that pushed me from needing into grieving. As it probably always is, I found it difficult to believe that my Grandmother, the only woman in my life, was gone from me. I couldn't comprehend the reality that I would never buy her tea for Christmas or buy her flowers or see her playing with our dogs.

Amidst all the crying and the grief, I felt anger. Twelve years suddenly seemed like twelve minutes. It should have been thirty-six years but my parents had stolen most of that from me.

Maybe everyone goes through certain chains of emotions during those times. I don't know. It was the worst feeling in the world.

I cried myself to sleep that night and cried myself awake the next day. Everyone in our home was in a state of shock and sorrow. According to my Grandmother, she had three grandsons. Even, our dogs, Goofy and Rufus could feel it.

One day, as I sat on the edge of the tub

in the bathroom to hide my outburst from others, Goofy walked in and sat right down in front of me. He scratched my leg to tell me he wanted to be held. A few moments later he was licking my face and I accepted his affection as a understanding.

I went to my desk and put in a CD that I had just bought. I put on my headphones and listened to Marina Belica (*October Project*) singing.

"One fine day, everything changes, in a moment. In her eyes, secrets of heaven, disappearing. In the silence, the yearning, turning to the earth. Forgotten. Long after tomorrow, only the wind will speak your name. In the silence, you'll be free of who you were."

At that moment, she was singing for me. I felt an acute presence of my Grandmother. I wasn't sure who the song was originally written for but the lyric, *"you'll be free of who you were,"* really got under my skin.

I thought about the times when my

Grandmother confided in me about the pain of her childhood as she was born with a cleft palate and what people then called a hair lip. I remember her getting emotional about her own father making fun of her for her speech impediment.

I also remembered her failing hearing and how she often looked pained when she felt she was missing out on conversation.

"Long after tomorrow, only the wind will speak your name. In the silence, you'll be free of who you were."

I sat at my desk and wept for an hour listening to that song over and over again.

The three days before my Grandmother's funeral were hectic and stressful. She had told me many times that she did not expect me to come to her funeral because of my parents. As much as I wanted to go, I knew my anger over my parents lack of visitation would become the only memory I would have of the funeral. So I chose not to go but decided we would go later in the year when there would not be any chances of turmoil.

Turned out that my decision was the right one. From the beginning of the planning stages for the funeral, my parents continuously worked to downplay the entire event. Instead of a respectful remembrance of her life, they chose a quick, church funeral, instructed everyone that there would be no flowers, no after service dinner and no traveling to the cemetery for a burial service.

"Grandma will be going to the cemetery alone." I was told that those were my mother's words to some other family members when they asked about the burial service.

The thought of my parents denying other family members the right to show respect to my Grandmother was almost more than I could take. Fortunately, Cindy, and other members from another side of the family, took over and made arrangements that my parents and sisters were neither aware of and of which they were definitely not a part.

Cindy took five flowers from the bouquet that my family of choice sent to the funeral and placed four of them inside her casket with her and took the fifth one for me and placed it in her hands. Showing that she would always be holding me.

At this point as I am writing this, it has been less than a month since all of this happened. My pain is still very raw and I am no where near finished with my grief. I don't think that will happen for quite some time.

In these weeks, since her death, I have returned to my peaceful life and have silently celebrated my twelve year old decision to walk away from my biological parents. Life is too short. I also recognized all of the things that my Grandmother did for me. Not just in the past twelve years but my entire life.

She might not have been able to spend time alone with me as a child but she did make every effort to reach out to me. It must have been unimaginable for her not to be able to spoil her grandchildren or take us places or do typical, loving things for us. But she kept trying anyway. No matter how many times my parents rejected her, she was consistently persistent.

It was that persistence that made her make me come out to her twelve years ago. It was that persistence that will leave me with no doubts about her love and respect for me.

In the twelve years of my relationship with her, she gave me the greatest gift possible, the gift of love. By loving me, she gave me the courage to love myself and, in turn, others.

Anything good, kind, and decent about me is only there because of what she not only taught me, but how she lived her life.

Being lost isn't so bad once you are found.

I believe I will love him more tomorrow
than I did today.
I wish skin didn't wrinkle.
I think he teaches me
how to love myself more.
I'm afraid I'm right.
I know what it is like to be lonely.

I believe that love will find a way.
I wish I didn't have to say goodbye.
I think God would stop the dying.
I'm afraid my biggest critics are those who have not
yet found freedom.
I know what it is like to be forgotten.